What Madness Brought Me Here

Other books by Colleen J. McElroy

Poetry

Music from Home: Selected Poems

Winters Without Snow

Lie and Say You Love Me

Queen of the Ebony Isles

Bone Flames

Fiction

Jesus and Fat Tuesday

Driving Under the Cardboard Pines

Nonfiction

Speech and Language Development of the Preschool Child

What Madness Brought Me Here

New and Selected Poems, 1968-1988

Colleen J. McElroy

Wesleyan University Press
Published by University Press of New England
Hanover and London

The University Press of New England is a consortium of universities in New England dedicated to publishing scholarly and trade works by authors from member campuses and elsewhere. The New England imprint signifies uniform standards for publication excellence maintained without exception by the consortium members. A joint imprint of University Press of New England and a sponsoring member acknowledges the publishing mission of that university and its support for the dissemination of scholarship throughout the world. Cited by the American Council of Learned Societies as a model to be followed, University Press of New England publishes books under its own imprint and the imprints of Brandeis University, Brown University, Clark University, University of Connecticut, Dartmouth College, University of New Hampshire, University of Rhode Island, Tufts University, University of Vermont, and Wesleyan University.

Some of these poems originally appeared in *Calapooya Collage II*, *Georgia Review*, *Nimrod*, *Woman Poet: The West II*, and these books by Colleen J. McElroy: *Music from Home: Selected Poems* (Southern Illinois University Press, 1976), *Winters Without Snow* (I. Reed Books, 1979), *Lie and Say You Love Me* (Circinatum Press, 1981), and *Queen of the Ebony Isles* and *Bone Flames* (Wesleyan University Press, 1984 and 1987, respectively).

The quotation in "How She Remembers the Beginning" by Milton Caniff is reprinted by permission of Nostalgia Press. Lines in "Learning to Swim at Forty-five" are reprinted from *Swallow the Lake*, © 1970 by Clarence Major, by permission of Wesleyan University Press. Lines in "It Ain't Blues That Blows an Ill Wind" are from "O to be a Dragon," from *The Complete Poems of Marianne Moore*, copyright © 1957 by Marianne Moore, by permission of Viking Penguin Inc. Copyright renewed 1985 by Lawrence Brinn and Louise Crane, Executors of the Estate of Marianne Moore. Lines in "Reports of Her Life Have Not Been Adequately Exaggerated" are reprinted by permission of Margaret Shafer.

Printed in the United States of America
∞

Cataloging-in-Publication information appears on p. 108.

Wesleyan Poetry

5   4   3   2   1

This book is for my family and friends, especially my children, Kevin and Vanessa. And for their hours of patient reading and sorting—a special thanks to the poets Frances McCue and Kate Gray.

Contents

from

Music from Home
Selected Poems

Sweet Anna Took Time

Snakes
shed skin,
a gentle thin
shell too tight for fit;
but ladies unfold.
Some bleed,
others find virginity
a state of mind.

Somewhere in the middle
of the war,
sweet Anna took time
east by northeast;
her buffle head
a seamless case of morals,
her slippery skin in smooth
black bulges
like the emerald and lime
shadows of sweet peppers.
A chambered vacuum.

Soft safe Anna
packed case after case
of bullets for the boys
who became men,
while Anna
became Sweet.

Somewhere in time,
the Allies invade
with case after case
of the dust she checked,
her velvet fingers flecked grey.
She sits facing east
in the light from these beaches,
the wire mesh window
shadows her face.
A setting for a folk opera.

Anna watches for the enemy
and listens to Mama's drone.
The boy checks the beach
as the voice ticks on;
his fingers weep
and he creeps through the mesh—
In one sweet hour
the battle is won.

In her net hose,
she hunkers
wet and sweet;
and when she packed for
nowhere
at war's end,
Anna could not be found.

So Sweet returned.
She keeps her bed
virgin clean
and patches her shell.
Somewhere in time,
her mind snaps shut
with a final dry
popping sound.

Webs and Weeds

Sidewalks of webs and weeds
Run parallel to empty lots where foul deeds
By handkerchief heads and winos were played,
To that old house where we stayed.
Irma Jean, Cora Jean and I, three debs,
Against the cracks of weeds and webs.

Sitting through matinees, dodging chores,
Chewing gum; claiming boys were bores.
But secretly grooming hair and breasts;

Jennie's brood, a female nest.
Irma, long-legged, delicious full lips,
Taught Cora and me to wiggle our hips.
George Darlington Love, a beau, my first;
They yelled his name like a tribal curse

As his virginal fingers pressed our bell.
Against that background of sights and smells,
We ignored switchblades, zip guns, and knees
Shattered by cops in that place without trees.
Now memories of dances are sprinkled like seeds
Among cousins and sidewalks of webs and weeds.

Sidewalk Games

I

The sidewalks were long where I grew up.
They were as veined as the backs
Of my Grandma's hands.
We knew every inch of pavement;
We jumped the cracks
Chanting rhymes that broke evil spirits,
Played tag at sunset
Among the fireflies and sweet maple trees
Or sang wishful sonnets about boyfriends
To the tune of whipping jump ropes.
The sidewalks wrapped around corners
Like dirty ribbons lacing the old houses
Together in tight knots;
Maple trees bordered
The all-white cemetery.
Sometimes we'd watch Priscilla's uncle
Sway down the dirt alley towards home.
We called her Pussy, called him
Crazy Max.
He was feebleminded and took to fits,
Barely making it from alley to pavement,
Loping down the street like a drunk.

We paced his jagged walk
Against tumbling tunes,
Taunting each pigeon-toed footstep
With rhyme.
The boys   bolder, louder
The girls   tagging along
Braids flopping like twisted hemp,
Ending in brightly colored ribbons.
We turned our black faces into silence
When he finally made it home;
Watched him grope up the broken concrete stairs,
Clutch the wooden railing,
Lunge for the broken screen door
And his medicine.
His tongue flopped wildly,
Parrot noises drowning his sister's cries
As she rushed from the black pit
Of their house.

One day, he leaned away from the safe umbrella
Of his sister's voice;
Leaned into the sky,
Hanging on the porch rail like a rag doll,
Then fell into the cracks of the sidewalk.
We rarely chanted after that,
Always passed Pussy's house in silence.
Sometimes I'd sit in the sweet stillness
Of Grandma's moldy basement
And draw his outline on the wet fuzzy walls.
The grey concrete backdropped my stick figure
As it fell into nothingness.

II

Bumpsy played the Dirty Dozens
As we jackknifed the length of the block,
Forcing grown-ups off the street.
We linked arms like soldiers,
Our black legs scissoring in precision.
    One's a company, two's a crowd
    Three on the sidewalk is not allowed —
    Last night, the night before

Twenty-four robbers at my door—
Po-lice, po-lice, do your duty
Make this boy stop feeling my booty—
Mary, Mary, tell me true
Who is the one you love?
Tin soldiers, wooden guns, and sharp tongues.
We got comic books for the price of one
In blitz attacks at Old Man Farrow's dirty store.
Garages were secret places for dirty jokes,
Our folks couldn't afford cars.
When we got older, we played house for real
Until we found Terry's baby sister's body
Behind a stack of tires;
The melodies we'd sung still seemed to bounce
Off the dirty walls and stacks of comic books.

III

Our houses ended at the sidewalk,
Whitewashed steps gleaming like teeth
Against the blocks of grey pavement.
We walked three blocks just to find
A vacant lot to feed Mildred's thirst
For green grass.
Fat Vaughn could eat a whole sheet
Of newspaper in less than three minutes.
Once, I licked the damp cellar wall,
But the taste didn't match the sweet smell.
Ten years later, I searched through Grandma's
Things before they were sold for auction.
I found her picture, three comics and the wind-up
Victrola we had used to put on our version
Of Cotton Club musicals.
We traded days so we could all be stars;
The rest sang chorus until the Victrola
Ran out of steam, the record moaning
Like a sick calf.
I found the stack of old pillows
We collapsed on, giggling and tumbling
Against each other like puppies,
While the needle stuck in one groove
Cutting circles in the records.

Recess

I come here alone   standing wet
and poetic in the rain
the school is still the same
dusty windows reflect dogs
stuck inside a chain-link fence
bricks smoothed by a thousand
tennis shoes and slamming doors
dull glass squares hide
rooms full of radiator smells
windows like checkered eyes
defying truants
in Sioux City, Biloxi, and St. Louis
I watch from the playground
and play out memories
each ghost a marble in my game
my new suede boots sound hollow
clumsy on these quick stones
I haunt friends

ten of us run blindly for a swing
kick a loose ball rolling by a line
of second graders   we're older, wise
even wiser now there are only six
four of us died
comics in a war for Captain Kidd
the rest prayed
stood in front of open graves
in wispy groups
like in the fifth
where we warbled long division
that the veins of my hands remember
when I lift a wine glass
to toast Virginia's last baby
her tenth   he lies too quiet in the crib
she stands as before
head leaning slightly to the side
at ten that pose would hide
pigtails as she stood at the board
wandering through prose rules
for saying things just so

she married Harry
always falling off his seat
smelled of unwashed socks
still does   smelled even worse
when he was shot by a cop

it's all there under the chalk dust
the Elmer's glue   x sum squared
and sandwiches stuck to wax paper
today's big dealer
sits between another war's hero
and a mother of ten
he picks his nose   she watches
the rain fall in wet strings
out there where I stand
wet   smoking   thinking poet
thinking   smoking in the rain

For My Children

I have stored up tales for you, my children
    My favorite children, my only children;
Of shackles and slaves and a bill of rights.
But skin of honey and beauty of ebony begins
    In the land called Bilad as-Sudan,
So I search for a heritage beyond St. Louis.

My memory floats down a long narrow hall,
    A calabash of history.
Grandpa stood high in Watusi shadows
In this land of yearly rituals for alabaster beauty;
Where effigies of my ancestors are captured
    In Beatle tunes,
And crowns never touch Bantu heads.

My past is a slender dancer reflected briefly
    Like a leopard in fingers of fire.
The future of Dahomey is a house of 16 doors,

The totem of the Burundi counts 17 warriors—
 In reverse generations.
While I cling to one stray Seminole.

My thoughts grow thin in the urge to travel
 Beyond Grandma's tale
Of why cat fur is for kitten britches;
Past the wrought-iron rail of first stairs
 In baby white shoes,
To Ashanti mysteries and rituals.

Back in the narrow hallway of my childhood,
 I cradled my knees
In limbs as smooth and long as the neck of a bud vase,
I began this ancestral search that you children yield now
 In profile and bust
By common invention, in being and belonging.

The line of your cheeks recalls Ibo melodies
 As surely as oboe and flute.
The sun dances a honey and cocoa duet on your faces.
I see smiles that mirror schoolboy smiles
 In the land called Bilad as-Sudan;
I see the link between the Mississippi and the Congo.

Horoscope

I am the October lady
Destined to live and die
In the first 31 days of Fall
I have more in common
With my lover's wife
Than with my lover
We float on the same sun sign
Check the Libra message
Watch us serve love/hate
Anger for breakfast
She is my sister

This will become
Increasingly clearer
Check Gemini and Aquarius

I am the intruder
Shaded, I curl tight
My sting kinked into
A black decimal point
I am zero, potent or helpless
Fused to an invisible screen
Hiding my head in its folds
Like one of Pablo Neruda's
Fantastic birds
Like the aril of a bittersweet
Time is on my side
My images of you are grotesque
I am devious and tantalizing
Let me help you wander
Through star sign, sun sign
Through orchestrations of planets
Lie low, act accordingly
You will know what I mean.

What Women Think About

a new man, no name
the body a melting weight
you think of
fresh mint love
fig sweet love
beyond the Song of Solomon love
daydreams for strangers
wicked and wise
wondrous as treasures
laid bare by shifting African deserts
you try saying it casually
even neutral words
are powerful as megatons

tested at White Sands
and you frail as the safety
in Eden's apple

his profile
curve of mouth
strong thighs
all add up to fine silk love
chiffon with strong perfume
thick sweaty armpit love
pungent honey sweet
cleansing and filling the pores
what few words you find
are whispered songs
erotic woodwind notes
with a few secret phrases
in Geez and Runic
that leave you mute
he walks into tomorrow
where another planet burns
the feeling goes with him
leaving you
and your memory
clicking like the change
in your coin purse

Pike Street Bus

Poem, we're going this way,
With that bus,
Its driver fat and full
Of unspent words like you.
Tell them about it, poem.

It starts this way,
A slow lumbering thing
Turning the corner.
Then the lead line drops.
The bus is stuck like

The driver's face
In the rearview mirror
As he watches sparks dance
In front of Pike Market,
Watches the line throw fire.
The broccoli's put away,
Apples gone, fish face sideways
In neat rows under a layer
Of white paper.
There's heavy breathing
On the bus.

The driver's face is swollen,
The grey evening settles
In lines around his mouth.
His belly peeks out, dull white
Where a missing button
Lets his shirt stand open.
He leaves the bus, catching sight
Of the lead line hanging
Toward the broken pavement.
A few faces turn to watch;
Others look sideways.
She stares straight on,
Her black face tired,
Her arms remembering forty offices,
Mop handle imprints still cling
To her palms. Her eyes are old
Before her time.

Say it for her, poem.
Tell her dreams of places
Where she's always young,
Smiling and sitting straight
Like the picture that stares out
From her dresser. She's crisp;
Caught by the camera alive,
In love, not knowing this night,
This bus.

Ignore the drunk that staggers on,
Lurching toward the coin box.
He hangs at an angle
Against Seattle's fading sun.
He leans back, falling
Into his past, using his coins
For balance before diving
For the slot; a handful
Of attention on his face
As the change drops.

Plunging toward a seat
Smashing against her feet
And dreams, his mind leaves
Him once again. She rubs
Her cleaning woman knees,
Stroking toward the pain on the floor.
Extra fat on her chin bobbing
As she remembers how she last saw
Her man; sitting barefoot
Atop a kettledrum, pounding
At an eight-hour day.

News Report

it's going to rain again
poets will scream of riots
and writers will research
mothers as if their black bellies
carried the billowy black clouds of storms
their fingers keeping tune for dull grey thunder

Mama, can we measure you on a Richter scale
are you unaware that the warmth of your arms
becomes hot winds, still and quiet before the rain
the tears you cried when your child
lay crumpled on the ground after the first tree climb
washes anger from crowded streets

or the slap of your hand against skin
for some childish trick finally stings
the roof of a prowl car with slick hailstones

is a satellite forecast
as bad as bringing home a note from school
and finally when it rains
will the poets quiet the world
with sweet words, as sweet smelling as wet spring

the tall thin sister swaying down the street
is unaware that she is a prairie wind
coiled tight, funneled into a high whine
tossing wheat and corn into the red frightened
face of a Kansas farm

a short chocolate lady tried fitting her bosom
into the confines of a bra, wincing
as the snapping band smarts her hand
flesh leaps from the folds, pushing air forward
and over, in forty or more turns
in Florida the force topples trees scatters
oranges into the sea, forecasters graph
the winds called She

the truth of such great gusts is gospel
and sung in mellow cocoa voice in storefront
churches, the satin lips of the sisters puff songs
sweet and low like the first movements blowing
Jamaica's shore before the tide is whipped unaware
into half an ocean or more, the froth
on those waves like lace cuffs holding good books
back at the churchfront store

a sweet chick smoking a cigar
sits beside a pocked kitchen table
crossing her legs, causing small gusts
noting quite seriously the pattern of coffee stains
on the floor, unaware that as a poet she must write
each line furiously before the wind shifts
toward another who takes a fancy to words

and now the verse before the sports report
a fuzzy map, out of focus dead center
jumbled highs and lows, degrees overview
curving arrows going not everywhere
swinging out to sea, lost
finding its way into a small town's
surprise like the young round girl
who carried roses to Maine in wicker
flower words to pollinate poems
until they are forgotten found
awaking some sleeping critic

from

Winters Without Snow

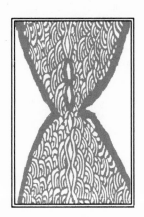

Memoirs of American Speech

1. From the Womb to the Tomb

you will learn to speak
just repeat after me
please
      thank you
           hello
your arms will move in 80° arcs
your tongue will click
without drooling
you will identify ships
in the harbor
   say it
       S.S. Ulysses
           Ticonderoga
          now
      slowly
you will know the meaning of color
  green grass
        good
true blue
       fine
black night
      red blood
stop
   it's not your turn
raise your hand only if you hear the sound
pay attention
move your head with your hands
try this
  MyFathersaysbaNanaNanaoil
don't stammer
        speak slowly
follow me
     you will need this
inhale   exhale
       watch closely
           count this
one thousand bars in this block

one hundred whores
you must make decisions
you must cast a shadow
let's say it together
          the policeman is my friend
the city's too pretty for death
this is a circle
                    this is a square
these blocks are all the same
speak clearly
                listen closely
once more
          after me
the baby is normal
                    normal

2. No Words Are Necessary

her husband beats her
he's thin as twine
his glands dried
from mustard gas
          aftermath
of a pimps and pushers war
he says she's country
but she won't speak

it must be subdural
her sentences clogged
from too much fatback
and beans
dry bread and butter
put her on a diet
drain the fat into tubes
stew out the juice

still no words
open the skull
rattle the cerebellum
crack it like a clam's shell
and pour in the nouns

the verbs will follow later
still grunts you say
she's too benign
her spine must leap and snap

each vertebra become
perfect as fresh new peas
submerge the torso
in heated baths
apply glycerine above the neck

electrodes please
the knife and the needles
find the switch   turn
the shock to full volume
trace the missing plurals
the system must respond

what   no answer   linguistically
impossible   code the dialect
plug in the computer
46, pregnant, mute and black
        we have no name
for this kettle of fish
toss her in the alley out back
mark no refund
on the welfare check

3. Stimulus-Response

when flames dressed the music store
in a gaudy cabaret of colors and smoke
I thought of news reports   night riders
bats and dancing bigots   how panic needs
the courage of sound   the hero's scream
before the charge   the fear of silent men
I remembered speechless children
the hours of painful sibilants
piercing narrow clinic rooms
remembered how I hissed   sharp and direct
between perfectly articulated teeth

I listened for guitars singing in the blaze
their strings stretching and popping
like petals of deadly red flowers
piano strings twanging in chorus
harmonicas screaming toward the melody
the wind drafts add riffs   but I cannot hear
I am glued to the sibilant crowd
we grind our teeth on the acrid air

we are drawn to the fire   awed
as any Neanderthal   its primal sounds
triggering our ancient ears   a signal
confusing the magic of words   reminding us
that death is the absence of sound
entranced by the flames
we are silent as deaf mutes   tomorrow
we'll play with coughs and grunts
groping for speech
understanding less and less

The Griots Who Know Brer Fox

There are old drunks among the tenements,
old men who have been
                              lost
forever from families, shopping centers
starched shirts and
                              birthdays.
They are the griots, the storytellers
whose faces are knotted and swollen
              into a black patchwork
              of open sores and
              old scabs; disease
              transforms the nose
              into cabbage   the eyes
              are dried egg yolks.
They grind old tobacco between scabby gums

like ancient scarabs rolling dung from tombs
in their
                              mother country.
In this country, they are scenic, part of the
view from Route 1, Old Town.

Don't miss them; they sit in doorways
of boarded houses in the part of town
nestled between wide roads named for
English kings and tourists.
                    These old men sit like moldy stumps
                    among the broken bricks of narrow
                    carriage streets   streets paved
                    with the Spirits of '76,
                    the Westward Movement and Oz.
These old men never travel the wide roads;
they sit in the dusk, dark skinned as Aesop,
remember their youth. They chant stories
to keep themselves awake another day;
                    tales of girls bathing in kitchens
                    before wood stoves, smells of
                              the old South.
                    Or Northern tales of babies bitten
                    by rats, women who've left them
                    or how they were once rich.
They'll spin a new Brer Rabbit story for a nickel;
tell you how he slipped past the whistle-slick fox
to become
                    the Abomey king.
But you must listen closely;
it moves fast, their story
skipping and jumping childlike;
the moral hidden in an enchanted forest
                              of word games.
                    These stories are priceless,
                    prized by movie moguls
                    who dream of Saturday matinees
                    and full houses.
You have to look beyond the old men's faces,
beyond the rat that waits to nibble the hand

when they sleep. The face is anonymous,
                              you can find it anywhere
but the words are as prized
as the curved tusks of the bull elephant.

Villanelle for Madness

Lady, your mind is turned raw side out
Watching dragons eat your birthday cake
Dropping penny arcade soldiers with one shot

Doctor, doctor, watch her slowly nibble suicide
A negative color packages her in a world of false pride
Lady, your mind is turned raw side out

An aging black sex trick; astrologically deep, yet lame
Sucked efficiently into an old fun house game
Watching dragons eat your birthday cake

Each candle is a man you wanted but lost
Those wet dreams that kept your reality in check
Dropping penny arcade soldiers with one shot

Fantasy is fake bat wings glued to success
You played to the hilt, snarling when you were hot
But lady, your mind is turned raw side out

Mama, your wisdom was not mother earth, not sweet
Just added guilt spots to the black lady's dream sheets
And she ages watching dragons eat her birthday cake

Full grown seeds from her black womb strike here paranoia hot
Ain't it alive, ain't it love, men are true, ain't it life
Lady, your mind is turned raw side out
Dropping penny arcade soldiers with one shot

Out Here Even Crows Commit Suicide

In a world where all the heroes
are pilots with voices like God
he brought her a strand of some woman's

hair to wear on her wing.
She looked sideways at the ground
silent behind the cloudy film covering

her eyes knowing she would be his
forever. They cruised the city nights
each one spiralling away from the other

but always coming home to gather stories.
Dark streets bright tavern lights drunks
filled with beer in the gutters.

The flicker of stars shaped like a hunter's
arrow bent stars that twinkled like babies'
eyes. No babies for them. She was an outcast.

He a loner. A perfect pair.
Winters had made him wise
And he avoided the single nests of summer.

He told her about things she could see.
How the dismal cover of clouds roils and explodes
and the ground aches like an old woman's knee.

How wood rots against the tide
good for hunting grub.
How to fade and fall back into the wind.

He translated her pulse
into near-language. Their poetry so personal
even Peterson's Field Guide could not tap it.

Only a stray hunter saw it.
Shook his head once thinking it a trick
of wind and wing then turned his eyes north

to search for the simple flight
of Brant or Canadian. Those patterns
he could easily understand.

That last night they drank from the river.
Sucked its delicate cusps of mold
sang anti social songs as if they were humans.

When he flicked his handsome head
to catch the drift of wind
she even managed a single tear.

She waited through days and nights
of grief. Circled the city less
then settled on the wires.

The metallic conductor captured her eyes.
She remembered how he proudly sang her name
as he pranced from pole-top to KV line.

One last fluff of feathers. One sigh
for all the unnested summers.
One single scratch

one electrical surge of power of love.
Then she fell smiling.
A trick he had taught her.

Breaking the Kula Ring

The Kula ring is a form of ceremonial trade used in the Trobriand Islands of New Guinea to establish intertribal relationships that last for years.

I am leaving the house
outside the landlord energetically
scrapes away old paint
I have passed a year
shedding a dozen neuroses

have been irritated by noise
food, the dull repetition of breathing
I have traded months of silence
with this house
the months like so many shells
of love and hate binding me to bargains
I cannot keep
now the cycle ends
the hours move counterclockwise
each month a precious circle of days
each day a fragile bead

the landlord has waited
through weeks of sunshine
it is cloudy today
and he paints frantically
slaps on coats of color
as bland as his urban mood
I have packed old clothes
tissue padded Xmas gifts
and stored away sad songs
like the one my daughter sings
of lost husbands and stray sons
her voice plaintive as a broken reed
wistful as the bent flowers
which the landlord has now decked
with drops of chemically sweet paint

he waves as we fall into pattern
behind the moving van
I think he is happy
his hand signals a cheerful good-bye
though I cannot see his smile
I turn away from his paint-flecked
ladder, away from the house
from the memories of laughter
and dreams, the unfinished metaphors
now trapped in hollow rooms
it is over, closed
like all the windows
the landlord has painted shut

Defining It for Vanessa

she is too young to eat
chocolates
they blossom on her black face
like peppercorns
she is 16 and dreams
of the alphabet stitched
to the winter wool
of teenage gladiators
in single capital letters
she leans across the table
and asks us older ladies
about love and the future
but we cannot see past
a few days at any time
we are pregnant
with memories
and move slowly
like Egyptian geese grazing

we tell her put Xmas
in your eyes
and keep your voice low
knowing this answer
as insane as any
will soothe her
while she dreams
wrapped like a mummy
inside her flowered sheets
she thinks we hold secrets
and watches us closely
as we shop for dried flowers
lovely center pieces
for the best china
we tell her smiling

later when we describe
our little aches and pains
she turns away
puzzled by antidotes

of blues reds and greens
we tell her how the reds
stick like anger
or clock the tides of the moon
we tell her how she'll guard
her lovely eyes
how only in her blackness
will she grow
large as the moon
we tell how women
with whiskey voices
will try to stop her
how men will strip her clean
of secrets
how the flesh hurts
how the world does not end
with the body
but the longing for it

To Whom Do You Wish to Speak

on the hour I begin
I am eight years old
thin as a spider
my dress is seersucker
I still hate it
he nods urging me on
lacing and unlacing his fingers
in exacting pyramids
I have an old tennis ball
no net no court no partner
I am black and lonely
the game is Irish
I play for hours counting O'Leary's
against the dull brick wall
the ball bounces rhythmically
to my tune
first the wall my hip my arm
a child's practice
for womanly gestures

he nods again
he has been trained to wait
to watch as I rush frantically
from one year to the next
in this black shroud of skin
I change and change again
looking for the me that is me
he says I must open doors
I tell him a husband story
a farm where cow tits
are colder than ice cubes
and love is the haymow
the wood stove
and dad's sweaty overalls
he is not convinced
he wants to walk through my memories
but I am lost and do not know the way

I stumble through the past
where images squirm like maggots
sightless mindless bodies
white and writhing in the muck
Victorian nightmares
as detailed as Brueghel paintings
or modern as Bearden collages
better yet
childlike and full of bright doom
but he is not repulsed
he asks for this
he wants to know the I that is she
forty-three minutes remain
sixty-second punctuations click
mid-story or silence
as the clock dumbly flicks
through another hour

I am walking home from school
the rag man smiles at me
he picks his way through trash
piled in dark corners of the alley
I follow his ugly back as he stumbles
past the crumbled bricks

I am ten and rubbish fascinates me
I give him a penny for the old garden basket
hanging from a nail of his pushcart
the wind is still nothing moves
I have yet to feel the bigot's cold cheek
but this man is black
and I know what he knows
I do not cry when his yellow teeth
bruise purple upon my lips
in the silence a little girl skips away
I become what I am
I am what I watch

now I ask if duality is the game of success
who can say what we are he frowns
this is she it is I
we are pronouns abandoned
by all nouns
I am the crazy lady escaping
from Sexton's poems
my house is on fire my children are gone
I am the lady in the bank without a check
the poet who forgot her lines
by day I sing in the first row
of the Church of Our Name in Christ choir
my flowered hat askew
above my black powdered face
I need no degrees for this
by night I ring the bells in Bedlam
I have no name
I am the forty-three-year-old masturbator
friendless and lonely
inside the poetry of Ai's *Cruelty*
grateful for the small taste of anything

he waits as I untangle a thread of words
I have sewn myself inside a web of rules
he promises nothing
like any good doctor he offers no omens
Thou shall not this
Thou shall not that
are reserved for mothers and priests

be patient he quotes
knowing I am the patient
the chameleon chasing myself
like the frilled gecko
I am the lizard who will not cast a shadow
wizened and tattered I slide among books
in search of honest secrets
a woman of letters
licking each metaphor clean
I supplement this diet
with the comfort of black earth
the coolness of black skin

I fumble and start again
tell him the one about dreams
there is a cave
the sun is a single eye
there are owls in the trees
they have ears
the bushes bear no fruit
I am twelve then twenty
now I have a lover now I don't
you touch me here
I touch you there
the world is white and electric
suddenly it is not
is that all he smiles
I answer him from still another face
there is no end, lies are truth
my life is without corners
we will move round and round
never closing the circles

from

Lie and Say
You Love Me

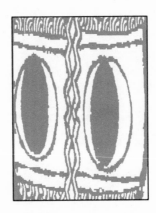

Tapestries

when I was eight I listened to stories of love
and etiquette while my mother's sisters
sat on Grandma's horsehair sofa
naked under their starched dresses
words flew from their fingers
in a dance as old as the moon
but I dreamed of other places
of dark bodies bending
to a language too dreamlike
and concise to decode

above them a tapestry desert stretched
into distant corners where I imagined
ancient rituals grotesque and graceful
conjuring up the moon-flecked
seasons of the earth
but my mother's sisters wove tales
that collapsed the world
into sarcastic snips of language
their black thighs opened
billows of powdery musk
rising from their legs like dust
from some raw and haunting land

I had a choice
two scenes their dark secrets
spread for my viewing
the usual desert palm trees camels
a cautious rug merchant one hand
on the tent, face turned towards the horizon
turning back like Thomas Jefferson
towards his black *anima*, like Lot's wife
or the thousands of black women
who fled slavery preferring instead
the monastic beds of the River Niger

it is said those waters flowed
red for years
shades of ochre fuchsia and russet

as layers of blood sifted
through the silt of the river
the velvet sands on that tapestry
were red and flowed into all corners
my aunts sat in a line beneath this scene
refusing to turn back
wagging their heads against the world's sins

I have seen more than my aunts dared to see
how each Sunday they sat bare-assed and defiant
their dark female caverns linking thighs
into matching hills of lemon ebony and mocha flesh
how the wooden humps reflected off my grandmother's
whalebone hairpins when she leaned into the light
the crumbling walls of the city of Benin
Kamehameha's feathered cape in the Bishop museum

I have seen Buenos Aires
where ladies dine inside their mirrors
Berlin where my blackness
was examined in six languages
Bogotá where there are no traffic signals
and even pregnant women are targets
fat clumsy figures playing toreador
with foreign made limousines

in the Middle East fairy chimneys
of volcanic tuffs spiral into the sunlight
their colors glowing like stained glass
in the half-light of the desert
shades of ochre russet and ebony
thrust into tidal waves of magma
and firestorm of ash
like beads on a rosary linking
village to village

when I was eight my prudish aunts
sat like squat pigeons on the horsehair sofa
brazen under their stiff-collared dresses
and I gathered dreams of love
from a tapestry woven in velvet

a blood-colored crescent moon, three palm trees
two burgundy camels, all arched around
a shadowy figure entering a tent
the world behind him barren and flat

some days pressed by the low ceiling
of a troubled sky I drift back to that room
the scene spreads before me
the delicate red tracery
of some ancient artisan
clinging to threadbare spots
the nomad who is forever coming home
the tent with its doorway of secrets
the dark face turned towards the corner
staring at some fixed point
on the amber horizon of that velvet desert
as if to say how vast
and naked the world seems to be

Caledonia

*Caledonia, Caledonia
What makes your big head
so hard . . .*

The way I hear tell aunt jennie
tapdanced on the hood of her husband's
car because she heard he *might*
have smiled at miz dora emma's daughter
Brand new ford baby pink it was
and a convertible right out of days
full of white buck shoes sock hops
and little richard wailing over the local
disc jockey all night party station
Neighbors whooped and laughed seeing her
fly straight out the front door swearing
that man would never live another day
seeing mama running down the block
just in time to catch her falling

butt first into the gutter
But mama wouldn't laugh because jennie
knew who had not accidentally put too much
red pepper in daddy's beans and rice
that night he came home smelling
of southern comfort and blue grass
neither of which mama ever touched
And who bought a one way ticket home
for uncle brother's first wife
stuck up and full of airs
just because she came *from* california
in the '40s before it was fashionable

Mama and aunt jennie both hardheaded
and lean on words
inhaling and saying humph and um-um-um
to a chorus of head wagging un-huh's
whenever they hear tell I'm having female
problems full of husband troubles
They have been married for as long
as anyone can remember and now so dependent
on their husbands and each other and husbands
on them and the other there's no telling
where one begins and ends
or which sister has religiously whipped
the other into shape
until I've learned that love, like hate
is always acted out

The Ways of Women

my cousins are sitting in the shadows
the flat light seems to nail them to the sofa
like overstuffed toys from a carnival stand
or matched bookends
like mother like daughter
they are round as cassavas
fat black and shiny

thick as those sweet lumps of licorice
I once bought in penny thin paper sacks
that always melted in St. Louis heat
they sit defining the world in total numbers of men
their plump fingers holding cigarettes
in a Casablanca pose
the toy poodle snaps at my ankles
while I pat my kinky hair into a smooth
cloud and tuck my feet carefully
under the chair

sooner or later they will remind me
of how frail I looked in cotton thin
dresses my fifth-grade books tucked
in the sweaty niche of my scrawny arms
I cannot remember all of their nicknames
they will not remember my last husband's
first name but sooner or later
they'll nod and tell me how my legs
were always too thin
and how they've stayed home to tend
mama's laundry and her nightly
gossip binges
they'll pull out their mink stoles
I'll show them my books
pictures of old lovers
we'll learn from each other

The Unkindly Finger of Junípero Serra

*Turn down the trumpets. This town was made
for the music of water.*
                              —Molière

he appears suddenly, white as an exposed
nerve, his profile wind dusted and blurred
his right arm jutting away from his shoulder

and ending in a point like an arrow
just where the road cups away from sage
brush hills and sweeps toward the sea

in the razor edge of sunlight
this could be Kansas or Wyoming
hills are bronze dried

and convenient as stage props
San Mateo rests in a southern
shaft of light that ends at the coast

Fra Serra kneels above the highway
his grey robes have been chiseled
from alabaster and hang in stony waves

like a soiled bridal gown
he has no family in sun or birds
flittering in hiccups of flight

about his great stone head
his feet rooted to these blonde hills
are too bulky and old world

too full of journeys made despite lameness
his thick finger points south and west
an accusing shadow falling into the valley

where farms end at the ocean's edge
and trapped in a river of lights, the great
middle class rush north and south

where towns are built for the music of water
and highways leading to pastel crackerboard
houses circle the cities like rings of Saturn

no one stops
not the children of those who pulled
this stone into place, not the Indians

those of his blessed flock who once stalked
this mission-filled land, not those who briefly
turn in surprise toward that commanding finger

like Hermes Quayro who keeps pennies under the corners
of his rug, and blind Santos who climbed the hill
to touch the plaque at Fra Serra's feet for luck

or Mary Lou Davis who dreams the statue into her bed
each night while her son plots robberies
in scores of houses ringing the valley road

Fra Serra exhorts them all
faces that carry the history of leather
the leitmotif of sand and cycles

tight-eyed girls who wear mean jeans
and thick-necked children whose laughter
swells the off-ramps of clogged intersections

leaning on one flexed knee
Fra Serra carves the horizon into a line
bisecting east and north: here he demands, here

and in the sunbaked light, in shadows
from fingertip to the rim of one great toe
where the land no longer rolls green into blue

his charges are washed clean by winds
and we forget the old promises
to cure blindness and lassitude

Why We Sometimes Paint by Numbers

for Pesha and Leslie

in 1958 in Kansas
wanting so much to be an artist
I painted the summer by numbers
from June to August
planted an indoor garden
threw the babies out of their room
laid a bedrock of crushed bricks
flushed gravel into the soil fill
then laced the next layer with charcoal
six weeks of calluses heaved top
soil in by the shovelsful
my onions were beginning to bud
when the house inspectors arrived

sometimes it is expensive to become
what we are
alive in that 2.4 house
with one husband and two babies
where women who so desperately
wanted love learned to hate
what I wished for was so private
I never saw myself standing
on the sheer edge of poems
or listening to the rhapsodic
circles of guitars
played to the echoes of mad Kansas
summers all trapped in livid colors
on a mad artist's canvas

the women we have known
are singing in the shadows
they are eating bits of light
savoring it on their tongues
like scallions or cloves
in the blue-grey of dusk
they swallow the dark
and grow thick as velvet

some come to this late in life
they learn never to trust
smiling children
they grow strong and do not fail
to mince sharp words
or share morsels of lost lovers

this is what you have learned
I have seen in your looks
that sweet secret women
give women when they know
all too well how things grow quickly
and madly and the electric
taste of flesh and loving ourselves
in the femaleness of it all
and how we fight the foetal
curl of old age
and how we have all ached
to throw dirt through a window
to build our own world
if for nothing but the onions

Looking into the Eyes

finally it is Gabriel Marquez's feet
this falling in love with book jacket photos
how writers hide everything
in metaphors of frowns as if contemplating
the separation of sky and ground
details that go unnoticed on crowded streets
are embellished by profiles etched
in the ebony and ivory
of chiaroscuro mystery
the way the head tilts determines
whether you will buy the book

you check poems against the slant
of nose and curl of lip as if

symbols unravel there hollowed
in the corner of the left eye as if
the chapter will somehow gain meaning
once that small scar beside the right
ear is properly highlighted and put
into humble perspective

backgrounds are filled with allusions
like images drawn from a sixteen-year-
old's dreams of how poets dream
look into the eyes
home is always some lonely country
or some lover's promise to return soon
features converge into anthologies
of lines until finally it is no longer
the face but the luscious curve of ankle
the arched toe the little one turned
inward coyly hiding some sweet secret

Lie and Say You Love Me

wake me for the good part
the takeoff is what I like best
droning motion and ailerons lifting
the sleeping space nuzzling
my years into numbness
until I break through cloud cover
emerging red as the sun

take the child that is me
into a primal desert
show me all oddities
one hump camels licking sand
from the eye of Osiris
scorpions and cactus that bloom
only in the purple green of midnight

make me believe
all manner of things
map city black streets
and watch me wander past beautiful
women who serve in circles of light
play a dance of tight feathers
for strutting male peacocks

and when I grow round with age
ribs drooping into midsection
paint a still life spectrum of red
feed me dreams synthetically laced
with beautiful words like mimosa
alliterative as horny authors

paint me intergalactic scenes
hand me my helmet and skintight suit
black velvet and weather-proofed
against time warp and cusp born writers
tell me this will last forever
know I believe it yes I believe it
all of it

The Lover Romanced by Rain

> . . . *oh, the bread of colleens butters the rain*
>   —D. Boucicault, "The Brides of Garryowen"

you and me
and a warm rain falling
Seattle rain
and my hair wrapped
in a tight scarf
the light falling
like polka dots
of green shadows
the pale scents of summer
dancing in a backdrop of trees

while each moment falls
into patterns of yesterdays

windowpanes of rain
and you covering the landscape
from here to the peninsula

today I am home alone
the rain has turned hard
and cruel as your laughter
the house is soaked and steamy
it smells dank and moldy
mud worries the doorway
milk turns sour with mildew
I found a moss-covered picture of you
curled like a dead spider
in the corner of a dark shelf
and the rain
singing like a sleeping pill

at night the rain is lonely
and calls me friend
I cannot remember what you called me

it has been raining for three months
rain falling without clouds
covering Elliott Bay in pale silver light
falling through a sudden haze of sun
and I hear the devil's wife
her moans synchronized to the beat
while blood showers of red rain
wash away footprints of dead souls
and cloak the night with singing stones

I no longer try to remember your eyes
I keep my room in the rainfall
of morning and open my arms
to the pulse of water
let tiny trickles wriggle like wet
fingers past my black belly and down
into the shallow cup of thighs
where I drown singing

it is always raining somewhere
whenever I dream of you
your face dissolves in rain

Reports of Her Life Have Not Been
Adequately Exaggerated

There she goes with her hands
in her pockets
She knows she's good
      Margaret Shafer, *Sleeping in Damascus*

And when she knew
He no longer loved her,
She began to love herself.
The bathroom scales said she
Had lost ten years at least.
Having courted the mirror
For more years than she
Cares to remember,
She now flirts with plain
Odors and home-grown scents,
Arranges a tryst
With her childhood,
Covers hours with a list:
    A teaspoon of wonderfully black
    Musical nights in a castle
    Where no one lives;
    Stew gently and call it home.
    Check the fruit for rot;
    You no longer need to eat
    Sins from checkbooks
    To bad weather in Tibet.
    Stuff a sweet tit for children
    With cornstalks and bitters;
    See how easily the eggs
    Separate from the yolk.
    When it is time for them to go,
    Without warning they do.
    Now add salt to the crust;

Scramble memories until no
Willows can weep for moon
Nights when the world is weedy
And floats like a wounded fish.
Each day she changes face,
Splitting herself away from all
Those roles she has owned
And the whispers of her reflection
In the pitted eyes of injured women.
Her body glimmering like a fountain,
She knits a shawl from her lover's lies
And no longer argues with the sun.
And when she grows old,
She grows very very smug,
Knowing she would have been a great
Fool never to have loved.

from

Queen of the Ebony Isles

Monologue for Saint Louis

home again and the heart barely there
when choked by clusters of words
thick as the clumps of blue-black
grapes we snitched every summer
from the neighbor's arbor
succulent pockets of flesh laced
with green staining our lips and fingers

it is summer again and I am home
vowing penance for all my disappearances
since that first summer
when the arbor was clotted
with pockets of grapes latticed on each
interlocking vine

now earthworms have trellised the arbor
and that crumbling heap of rotting black
sticks cannot shield us from wind or words
we are the women we whispered about each summer
familiar houses and schoolyards have disappeared
childhood streets are blocked with singular black

one-way signs aligned like a lacework
of warnings or accusing fingers
I am home again
and my cousins sit in their cloaks of black
skin dragging me through twisted vines
of genetic maps thick with childhood vows

they remember each summer
how each year I vowed to return home
forever but I am lost in a riddle of words
home is a vacant lot its backyard clotted
with a stainless-steel arch and clusters
of tiny parks sprouting like trelliswork

enclosing some strange summer
resort my cousins have disappeared

into like the shadows of beasts and bad air
that infect this flat country and I am home
a stranger in love with words
with tart sweet clusters of poems

Ruth

And Ruth said . . . Intreat me not to leave thee, or to return from
following after thee; for whither thou goest, I will go . . .
                                        —Ruth 1:16

it took 27 years to write this poem
27 years mama and still I see you falling
like a lump of coal down a chute
arms hands and feathered thighs churning
inside a tumbling hulk of helpless flesh
falling away from me
your dress flying open
until you were finally free form
and without face

since then I have counted those stairs
I would like to say there were 27
but significance lies not in exactness
but in the panic of not knowing
which step would claim you
I have saved that morning
the blood-sucking thud of body
against wood   the back staircase
of that red brick duplex
where you clawed air

we had fought   I remember that
about what   nothing
grandpa's untimely death
my 16-year-old womanish ways
how someday I too would flail
at my own daughter
so many fights   so many stairs

and you tumbling as my terror
claimed me like Venus
without arms or legs to stop you

one moment you were larger than life
your black arms spread like the wings
of some great vulture   the next a step
missed and you fragile   distorted   plunging
in wingless flight toward some evil nucleus
waiting in the space below the steps
but we cannot go back
I cannot correct that split second
when I failed to lean forward
bodies will not reverse and tumble
upward   unwinding into familiar forms
limbs intact   I have hesitated too long
and the landing is too crowded

what dusty things we would find there now
how you quoted Shakespeare for every event
from slamming doors to Sunday walks and bigotry
a broken lamp   your jealousy and mine
too many unspoken holidays
for your one daughter too many
or too many husbands for one daughter
how your senseless plunge into a void
showed me more than all your ominous warnings
how the cycle of blood and pain
has brought us both to this childless time

I have finally faced myself in you
for years I have written poems nonstop
but yours were always more difficult
I have even tried dream language
but your image slips into some zone
of blackness even deeper in color
than your skin when I angered you
how often has the venom from your blueberry
lips stunted the growth of a poem
how often has your voice been with me
wherever I go   you have gone

and sometimes gladly my need to reach out
has pulled you to me
mama for years I have hidden
hundreds of unfinished verses
in the corners of dark closets
read this
and count them

While Poets Are Watching

for Quincy Troupe

Harlem is on parade
recalling St. Louis
as if like us
the whole scene
has been transplanted here
Stanford White's window offers
remnants of James Van Der Zee's world
it is filled with urgent gospels
infecting us both with memories
of our common birthplace
I see you take notes
always the poet
but in the dry space
where I have stored words
pictures from this Harlem window
kaleidoscope faster
than any pen will move

you have to come back you say
this is rich and heavy
like good food
you say here
are our poems
smiling as your next words
are drowned in tambourines
and harsh songs of salvation
blasting from loudspeakers

lampposted below the window
for a moment the hymns
from the corner tabernacle
outdrum the cadence
of the parade

this is the third Sunday
in August and thirty-second-
degree Masons
strutting like crested pigeons
swell the black heart of this town
we watch from the window
matching faces with memories
the skinny old woman next door
praises the past
like any good church lady
she is powdered like a turn-
of-the-century matron
her sunken black cheeks
dusted with pale blue, ivory or rose
to match pastel dress, stockings, shoes
you take note chanting
come back, come back
this is home and love

we are poets watching
tight-hipped black girls
swing their batons
to the high-step
rhythms of vaseline-smoothed legs
while the oompahs of school bands
count march time for drill teams
we watch until dusk
until the bands
grouped like gaudy flowers
have played their last notes
until the old men have
placed their calloused feet
on the nearest footstools
and the girls have gum-chewed
their mothers into silence

these faces are familiar
as Van Der Zee's photos
as my mother's snapshots
of cookouts in Uncle Brother's
backyard or your own scrapbook
of our high-school homecoming
it is all predictable
from the street smells
of old whiskey and urine
to the sun fading
against Columbia's canker-
green roof
we are home, coming back
always coming back

From *Homegrown: An Asian-American Anthology of Writers*

for Bee Bee Tan

I have seen this picture before
usually after a war
it is always faded brown-grey
and slightly burned around the edges
the composition is much the same
eyes full of innocence trying
vainly to guard young bodies
the boy in front is the leader
and the couple there
deliberately not holding hands
are lovers
they are all poets

they are always standing on the stairs
of some building where accordingly
they learn by generation
what lines have brought them there
the sun always washes
their various sizes with a hopeful blur

they are always the ones who want
to knit the old country to its children
and they are the ones who steal for a free
breakfast bags of oranges and cookies
for preschoolers and old ladies
who smile their appreciation

this picture holds names that are Asian
but it is much like those I've seen
on reservations or one my mother has
of me near Selma with friends
from my all-black high school
or maybe my younger brother
before his uniform was official
in this picture and the others
it is the last recognizable day

before the hills take what we know
to be our childhood
and that girl on the right will
no doubt walk a barefoot snow trail
to death and the intellect will
gain hostility with each
point of lost logic
and the writer will find
no metaphors in bullets
and their own people will
finally understand them even less
than the rest of the world

A Triangle of Sun Temples and Lost Lakes

1. Among the Sun Temples

These mountains are like women.
From a distance they are soft, graceful and willing,
Their skirts neatly arranged
As if they are following some pattern.
These stately ladies

Attended the River of the Sun
Even before it gained its name.
From Pachácamac to Sacsahuamán
They have embraced Quechua and Inca,
They are willing to embrace you.
Like mothers they will harbor you,
Bring you fruit, bread, the juice of rare leaves.
They will shelter virgins
And shove strong boys into manhood.
At night you can sleep
In the crevice of their bosoms.
They will whisper strange stories
Of the moon and stars
But do not trust them,
They will pinch your ears
With the pain of thin air
Or drown you in crystal-clear waters.
They have conquered gods
And men who would treat them like midwives.
Yet they always beckon,
Sucking the wind into their cleavages
In a lonesome harlot's song,
Their tawdry green dresses
Full of sensuous mystery.
They have been kissed by centuries of history,
By Inti, Sinchi and jewel of Quechua.
They are called all mountain—all peak,
Navel of sun god, flesh of inner earth.
And while they hold the surprise
Of innocent young daughters,
They have grown hard as adulterous wives.

2. After the War of Lost Lakes

Under a soft celestial quilt
The beggars outside Lima
Curl up in the warm dust of yesterday.
Though it smells of lost lakes and llamas,
Strong warriors and the bowels of ancient gods,
It does not close out the cold mountain air
Or memories of the great halls of Machu Picchu,

So they buzz like ragged hummingbirds
Against the pale rims of small bonfires.
On the Urubamba they were keepers
Of lovely women and sun-blessed kings.
Now a ten-gauge railroad
Zigzags through their dreams
While church bells peal in chorus.

They sleep in layers,
The old ones nearest the cobblestones
Their eyes falcon sharp
And bloated with hunger,
Their bones brittle as Pizarro's
Whose parchment-colored corpse
Is preserved at even temperature
Inside the cathedral behind them.
These are the true relics of saints,
These gaunt creatures who beg
In the shadows of trees,
Whose ancestors carved their names
On the bloodstained walls of catacombs.
Here in the square where geography is locked
In pottery, bones, and snakes,

Their tortured past has been made
Part of the national monument.
This is the legend.
It is in their eyes
And each morning when they arrange
Tattered pieces of their history
Into gaudy tourist patterns,
Then welcome the sun
Back to the town
They still call Pisac,
You can see them jangle
Their conquerors awake
With a vengeance.

3. Mirrors in Ecuador

Today we leave for Otavalo—
We will shop for emeralds, ruanas,

And bread-dough figures of Christ.
The weather here is home—
A macramé of lakes knots valleys to mountains.
In the crevices towns spread like plankton.
This is a northwest scene painted Spanish.
We will consume its treasures.
On each corner we will capture street vendors.
Every morning they blossom like bright flowers,
Their birdlike chatter
Filling the spicy air.
Behind their shields of humility
They sing out to us—
For you, madame, this is special.
This is the offer for which you will pay.
You will smile when clever natives
Swallow your money like aspirin.
I season my peppered nerves with poetry
While the others shield themselves
Behind cameras and zippered bags.
My skin offers no shield.

Here among Pasalaquas, Mestizos, and Creoles
I am too much at home.
Here where the rain blows
Into the hollows of sun-ruffled valleys,
Where hillsides dip and swirl like green velvet
Or wrinkle like the fleshy thighs
Of huge dark women,
I watch my twin barter for gold.
In the liquid shadows her blackness is familiar—
But I am called madame
And for her I am special.
When she praises my one-line Spanish
Her eyes are hungry for dollars.
She is Esmeralda selling tribal dreams
Of green fire—
She has been here before
And knows the power of bargaining,
But all I see in the space between words,
Between drops of rain
Is how we are both sad
In any language.

What the Red Flag Means

This is no Spanish dream
In this town, they glean rough wool into rugs
Madonnas are carved from sandalwood
Their smiles eternally fragrant
The red flag signals fresh meat
And the thick sweet smell of blood

Peasants and gentry surge
Toward the town's center
Their smiles glazed by the odor
Of entrails and sinewy muscles streaming
In the sunlight of the butcher's doorway
I am trapped in the marketplace

Caught in a funeral procession
For some third grader
Who stood too close to the blade
The bull's head lies on the cobblestones
The child's face still trapped in its eyes

This is how they do it
One smooth cut
And the crowd licks at Spanish words
For life and death
While mourners weave past
Like cherubs in school clothing

The wood-carver works faster
Chips falling to the dirge
Of a dozen tiny feet as he whittles
Precise contours of the casket
Miniature faces, the bull's head
The cup and curve of Peruvian mountains

The red flag wavers, is still
And behind the cracked shutter
Of the last house on the square
A black face stares at me
Under this dull Peruvian sun
Our eyes will not hold

The soft curl of the carver's blade
We still remember diaspora
Conquistadors and human heads rolling
And how we've both arrived here
All at once and at the same time

This is what the red flag means
My black face even darker
In the shadows of this town
That other face caught in a window
While on the end of the blood-raw neck
The bull's head swells inside
The green mold of death

This Is the Poem I Never Meant to Write

my grandmother
raised me Georgia style
a broken mirror
spilled salt
a tattered hemline
all add up to bad spirits
when she died, I learned to worship
stranger things
a faded textbook full of bad theories
has no spirit at all
now I've gone full circle
in a town some still call Bahía
the drumbeat of the alabés
echoes my grandmother's warnings
I watch the daughters of the candomblé
dance to the rhythms of ancient spirits
as the ceremony begins
my lungs expand
like gas-filled dirigibles
stretched latex-thin

my grandmother spoke
the language of this scene

the mystery and magic
of rich colors in a tapestry
of brown and black skin
white candles
a small reed boat
six bloody gamecocks
all bind this church to its African source
I follow my people past spirit houses
past tight Spanish streets
where houses are painted blue and white
like any Moorish town
when we reach the sea
water seems to flow uphill
tropical landscapes turn mustard yellow
and above us the moon swallows the night

this is the poem
I never meant to write
I am learning to worship
my grandmother's spirits
an old woman
splinters of wood embedded
in her black leathery cheeks
three crosses tattooed
on the fleshy black skin
of her upper arms
draws my picture upon her palm
in blue ink
then tells me we are all strangers
bound by the same spirits
I have gone home
in the dim light
my grandmother smiles

Queen of the Ebony Isles

this old woman follows me from room to room
screams like my mother   angers like my child
teases me   rolling her tattooed hips forward
and out   steals my food   my name   my smile
when you call her I come running

when we were young and perfect
we danced together and oh we loved well
all the husbands and lovers   children and books
the sunshine and long walks on lonely nights
now she sucks me thin with her affairs

weaves romantic shadows over the windows
and curses my sober moods   kisses everyone
and insists on wearing red shoes
she hums the same songs over and over
something about love and centuries turning upon us

each time she changes the verse
shifting the words like cards in a game
of solitaire   the hot patent-leather colors
her mercurial moods as she flies about
her red heels glittering and clicking out of tune

she has seen too many comic strips
believes she's as deadly lovely
as Dragon Lady and Leopard Girl   I resist
but her limbs are daring   oiled for movement

without me who are you she asks   I am heavy
with silence   my hands are maps of broken lines
without her all sounds are hollow   I am numbed
cold and cannot read the cycles of the moon
even the sun   the sun cannot warm me

aloneness is a bad fiddle I play against my own
burning   bet your kinky muff she cackles knowing
the symptoms   then draped in feather boas
she drags me toward yet another lover   beckoning
with her brash reds pulsing like haunting violins

on midnight-blue nights she screams
into the eyes of the moon   twirling her war machine
like some kamikaze pilot   her heat bakes my skin
even blacker   she's never happy unless we're falling
in love or hate   she grows younger while I

age and age   bandage wounds and tire too easily
she says   play the game   play the game she says
when I complain she says I'm hearing voices
she's hacked my rocking chair into firewood
I am the clown in all her dreams

when she looks into the mirror from my eyes
I want to float away unscathed
drift like patches of early morning fog
she thinks I stay because I love her
one day soon I'll move while she's sleeping

The Ghost-Who-Walks

none of this makes any sense
not if you consider
what you really remember
not the name of the high yella
snooty kid third row front seat
who sat like an eraser
September to June for three
grades with her clean name
long hair and starched shirts
and your mama called her uppity
and all you can remember
is how often the teacher called
her and how you hated
the way she made your sad
face seem dirty

so why should you remember
some cheap comic hero

who never looked like any man
you knew then or since
or could talk to or sing to
those silly songs
about freckle-faced
sweethearts who never lived
on your block or wars
you never fought
or black folks full of voodoo
that made your gramma laugh
and throw salt over her shoulder
or women who pined and waited
for men like you
never have or will

none of this has anything really
to do with the way bright-
eyed children gather shadows
of words and make pictures
and run with them
the way the Phantom ran from Sala
to Diana and back again
and how he always said
darkness was good and goodness
was light and the pygmies
howled and cringed and he
marked his victims with a skull
which we all have

Lothar's Wife

he's only a smart-ass when he's home
with Mandrake
he's silent and obedient as a snail
his bald pate bowing into the cape's
trail and dreaming
of tales he'll bore me with
his one night home

once a month
that's what I get like clockwork
and always on the full moon
half my allowance he reserves
for sheets, tearing them with his teeth
to vent the forced silence
of those other twenty-odd days

did I say odd
it's that one day that's odd
his coming home full of half-tricks
he's picked up from the master
the hypnotic hunger
he so willingly tries on me
he claims he stole me, bought me

claims he's Zulu, Bantu, Beja
depending on the hour, day, or year
says I was the black spot
in the white of his eye
the speck he turned into leopard
that unwittingly turned into woman
neither of us no longer knows what's real

and my mother beats her fat tongue
against her gums
as each month I try to reveal the puzzle
stroking the lines from his hairless
obsidian crown
I hear her rumbling around in the next room
I soothe his sweet head and she moans
heaven protect us from all the things
to which we can become accustomed

How She Remembers the Beginning

*You remember a bad gal longer than a good one. The only women
who get their names in history books are those who ruined empires
or poisoned a whole bunch of guys.*
   —Milton Caniff, *Terry and the Pirates:*
      Enter the Dragon Lady

I woke up just in time to clear my throat
it was like the ending to an old rerun movie
the hero had been buried
one engine conked out over the Aleutians
shrimp had stopped feeding on the west shore
and some fool was trying single-handedly
to clean up Harlem
I materialized in one complete stanza
a distortion of memory like a séance
of poetry or a broken record playing
Angel Baby again and again
an inscrutably haunting tune
warbling against a cracked needle
I became a hustler a thief
stole these lines from old dusty comics
I found in an abandoned barn
stole them all from a time when dreams
were medicinal and the world was full
of mystery and love

but this is only a fragment of my story
originally my plan included saving the world
now I must save only myself
empires have risen because of a woman
and fallen for the same reason
a Dragon Lady recognizes her weaknesses
only sentiment can lower the iron mask
of my reserve—there is of course an escape
one night when the fog is at its peak
I shall slip the cowl of my black cape
low over my eyes
and when I'm too far away
for him to remember how my hips
melt into his hands

I'll write a letter unsigned
disguising the way pain
has drawn my lips into a cruel smile
or how I must now use men
for what they are
and never what I imagined him to be

The Dragon Lady's Legacy

years later, they could hardly remember her face
then a farmer plowing a tired field of soybeans
and lentils near Half Moon Bay
found her pearl-handled revolver
in a sump by a forgotten wellhouse
silt slid from the curve of metal
like folds in a silk dress and her initials
filled the dreary light with promise

for days, he carried the secret in his pocket
then his dreams infected his wife
she saw fires scorching the villages
in the valleys below them
the smell of strangers grew thick as napalm
and a slit of light, crafty as a woman's sigh
suggested battles yet to be planned
somewhere in the night she heard the lady speak

your breath will pulse in strobe-light patterns
of eight, she whispered
two for your husband and unnamed children
one for this house teetering
on its crumbling foundation like a child
one for that useless fence and barn
another for your sisters in other ghettos
the rest for yourself arising
gloriously, finally a rebel
alive outside yourself

each night, the lady returned
the farmer bathed himself in tales of love
where he was the hero
his wife pressed her onion-stained fingers
to her ears and begged for the old loneliness
the days pale as thin soup
the brief spate of evenings
still she saw the variegated shadows of sandalwood
so surprisingly delicate the lady took shape in them

her razor-sharp nails glistening like diamonds
come follow me, she said
it is an old story so foreign
it is typically Middle American, as always
when it is finally released to the public
everyone from lawyers to victims
will be FBI agents
but you are full of long-limbed seduction
and have nothing to fear

even now, soothed by the swell of adventure
there are those who say the lady is a myth
in these days there is no siren's voice
to lure men into battle or women
from the quicksand of supermarkets
there are no ladies of iron will or dark mysteries
and when you have settled into the safe corral
of your routine, *do not be deceived*
by the faint scent of our perfume

from

Bone Flames

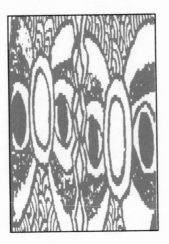

Learning to Swim at Forty-five

I could not whistle and walk in storms
along Lake Michigan's shore . . .
I could not swallow the lake.
    —Clarence Major, *Swallow the Lake*

Having given up hope for a high-wire act
I've taken to water and the quicksilver
Danger of working words hand over hand.
At the edge of the pool I am locked in gravity
And remember the jeers at Girl Scout camp
Where *catfish* meant anyone who lived in a ghetto
With no pools and no need to tan and everyone
Spent more time learning how to keep their hair
From *going bad* than they did learning breaststrokes.

And yes, Clarence, I learned to swallow the lake
Including all that it held and what I was told
By Mrs. Fitzsimmons of Harris Stowe Teachers
Who later said I couldn't hold the elements
Of tone or the way words break and run like rain,
The *Hecates* and *Africs* filling the page
Until it grows buoyant under the weight of sonnets,
A feat she believed so unconsciously automatic
It arrived full blown at birth.

For forty years I've lived under the pull of air,
All the while knowing survival meant learning
To swim in strange waters. *Just jump in and do it*
They yelled at camp, then tossed me heels over head
Their humor an anchor dragging me down.
There I defied training films and descended just once,
My body stone weight and full of the first primal fear
Of uncurling from the water belly of a mother country.
There I could not whistle in the face of the storm
And even my legs were foreign.

Poetry like swimming cannot be learned
Fitzsimmons insisted as I rubbed the smooth skin
Behind my ears where gill flaps had failed to appear.
Now years later, I voluntarily step below the surface

And there beneath the chlorine blue, I am finally reptilian
And so close to the Middle Passage, I will pay any price
For air. If silence has a smell, it is here
Where my breath fizzles in a champagne of its own making,
Where I must learn to sing to the rhythms of water
The strange currents and patterns of moons and tides.

Fitzsimmons, it doesn't happen all at once. To swim
You must learn to labor under the threat of air lost
Forever and hold fear close to you like a safety net.
You must imagine the body, the way it floats and extends
First like an anchor, then a lizard or a dead leaf.
Direction is some point where the sun is inverted and sweet
Air hammers the brain with signals that must be ignored.
You learn to take risks, to spread yourself thin,
You learn to look *through a glass darkly*
And in your darkness, build elegies of your own rhythms,
And yes, Fitzsimmons, you learn when to swallow
The lake and when to hold to the swell of it.

Years That Teach What Days Don't Even Know

> sold to the highest bidder for three
> hundred dollars, all of my grandma's
> life put on the block beside

> buttermilk cans, beer bottles, wooden
> matches and sales receipts from Kresge's
> dated circa our-time small-time USA

> sold and I learn black folks have antiques
> which leaves me wondering what is peddled
> second-hand in Tangiers, Antwerp, and Peking

> stuff designated ancient by idiot aunts
> too much like my grandma's oldest girl
> soothing her need to physically
> maul somebody's history if not her own

sold for three hundred with all
my memories of songs that loved me
when I was down and knew nothing but blues
and honky-tonk playing grown-up sad
beside the roll top desk Grandpa ferried
upriver on a flatboat in 1901

sold to fill warehouses already full
of dynasties, families and kingdoms
enough for entire museum lines
of throwaways like self-service quick
stop trays from White Castle dime
burgers to silver-foiled super macs

sold and twenty-three years later I see
Grandma's dresser cluttered with photos
of bustle-skirted sisters like sepia Renoirs
and her chiffonier, tiffanies, and roll-up
Victrola which colored folks naturally
couldn't really own owing as to how

all that stuff is junk anyway
and ripe to be sold by doddering relatives
or smart-ass kids who never dream
of cliff-side high-rises on islands
like Runu or Yap or what some scrawny
pioneer woman left on the stoop in the rain

where I sit crying over the loss
of pictures showing Uncle Roman's second
wife in a plumed hat and a dark smile
shirt-waisted right up to her chin
or another faded print of that ash-black
zoot-suiter who called me "cuz"

these are my years, so give them back cause
dead or alive they're how I learned
the proper tense of verbs:
to be, to have, to own

To Market, to Market

on the levee the smell of smoked
fish separated me from my ill-earned
allowance quicker than the cheap ropes of red
licorice and packets of tart Koolaid
my St. Louis cousins constantly craved—
under the glass-domed market, everything imitated
'what someone else had dreamed and square-tucked
into paper cartons, pure white as city fathers planned
but I was black and Catholic and needed a life made
possible by the brine of open seas and mysteries of finned
sunstreaks dancing on green oceans, a world I feared
and loved, fascinated as my grandma hummed
songs of Jesus' wealth while she beheaded
catfish or filleted carp already scaled—
at ten I almost knew how fish could hold a deep-seated
sense of magic despite man's prehistoric dread
of salty graves and red tides, so I traded
with gill-faced fishmongers who snickered and palmed
50¢ for half-spoons of fish eggs or lox glued
too thin to sheets of waxed paper, and later bus-bound
for home, my crimp-haired cousins wrinkled
their fat black noses and refused
to sit near me—   "You were weirded
out," my daughter announces now when I feed
her tales of how even then I had a strange need
for the smelly magic of the sea, its fruit and tides—
water singing of countries yet to be tasted

Putting My Son on Board the *Columbia*

Each time home, you vow never to return north
Where every winter is always darkness.
You try ignoring the house you've missed, announcing,
"If it weren't for the sun, I'd always be lost,"
Your eyes taking on more coldness than I imagined.
Your world has finally become imagination:

Six months imagining home and the other six
Remembering how quickly age comes in the Aleutians.

You were the only black aboard a ship heading
Into a series of too many Alaska good-byes.
Since that first trip you have taken on the act
Of returning as if you were storing winter garments.
Each day home, you hand me stories of boys
Drifting too quickly into men as you reach
Toward me for the ease of your own childhood,
But I can only see your face growing toward
Your great-grandfather's bony angularity.

You told me how baby crabs and octopi slip
Into crevices on factory ships between deck and bulk-
Head like wet laundry or old jello-colored sea kelp,
And in telling, pulled your hands, jerking them free
Of imaginary snare-hooks as you explained how tentacles
Were glued for days to any surface that held firm,
And how fishermen chopped them out, cursing.

"A quick thump between the eyes stuns them," you say
And I see how stunned you are to find home changed,
And how you've learned to live in a world where fish
Drown and you silently curse what glues you to the sky
Above this house where good-bye, good-bye never grows
Any better than that first time you sailed the *Columbia*,
The shadow of an adult just barely fixed to your face.

You say, "Sometimes octopi take forever to die
Out of their element—they don't know when to let go
And by morning, they're spread tentacles-wide on the deck."
You tell me how you grab them while they are still
Dazed and how you can never look them in the eyes where
You swear the mother sea is always moving, green and cold.
Then you take me by the shoulders and shake me to laughter
Saying, "Com'on, Mom, this won't hold water and I'm no Matthew
Henson—just another black kid making bucks off the sea."

Yet by late night, you'll tell me how you threw them
Into the Bering Strait and how you hoped they'd know home.
That's when your face grows soft and you shower
For the fourth time that first day,
Trying to get the smells out.

Song of the Woman Who Knew Too Much

The land is cold and its men gather earth for no reason. Their eyes fail to give
   them pictures of the inner world. They are angered by small changes
   in clouds.
I am Diamonane, daughter of seven voices, my language as old as soft hands across
   a man's bared chest. Bones mean nothing. It is the flesh, hot and
   sweet, it is there you flower and die. You have seen me walking
   slowly at the edge of foreign seas, you have seen me choking on diesel
   fumes of cities, eating muskmelons under the striped tents of incense-
   filled bazaars, quarreling with the fishhawkers in the French Quarter,
   or standing, head bowed, at the edge of a clearing among Dutch settlers
   in those first New England snows. But always, always, my cape, full
   and black, billows and flows even on windless nights.
My father weeps like his father before him. He weeps for fathers yet to be born.
   He has seen the zebra die, watched the blood bubble and spurt from the
   severed head like blue gas from an open pit of volcanic earth. Blood
   erupting with the swift touch of an ubaba's blade, a chieftain's weapon,
   definite and deadly. My father knows this ritual sings of other
   treacheries, the whispered trading and bartering of bodies that split
   men from their countries and bloat skinny jungle trails with long coffle-
   chained rows of people who could build a great nation.
My father knows that the dull eyes of the dying zebra will be repeated until both
   chieftain and farmer pray dumbly to new gods. The lovely blue waters
   of the Bight of Benin hold a body for three days before it's washed out
   to sea, Dachau is eleven miles from Munich, and the slave castles of
   Madagascar cannot be seen from the shores of Mozambique.
My mother was the first Eritrean, too noble and proud for deserts. She abandoned
   me in the courts of Messinessa and Syphax, sent me to Carthage where I
   stayed until Hannibal arrived. Later I fled, and still later sang
   frail lyrics to the strings of Te-kwa-ta's knee harp in the courts of
   Ann Zingha, warrior queen of Matamba. I was well groomed for my role,

knew the subtle costume, the changes in skin, knew the snake-sly eyes
of the dancing woman and the cow eyes of the wifely woman. I was
sold for a high price and willingly loved my king.
I have known time and halcyon days. I have learned to pick my wounds like a wild
bird and to feed on berries in the kingdom of Kotoko. I have run with
the antelope and spoken to the griots. Those wily-faced half-men and
she-apes have chased me into the clearing, damned me for living like a
poet, and forced me into marriage rituals.
Once I rowed from a Roman galley, its sails bellowing out like brim-filled wine
gourds, its belly full of women, black like me and framed in fear.
The Roman, Theallus, keeper of the osprey, cradled and kept me in a
coffin of tiles and sickly perfumes. He loved me too well and was put
to death when I left. I still see his eyes, sad and dark as the
polished wood of the oud. I conjure up his image in songs that command
the strings of the oud, and like Tě-kwa-tǎ's knee harp, the oud sings
melodies of death as sweetly as a child.
I have bathed in my father's loins and he has called me quela, bird girl. I have
loved daughters and sons, licked the hollows of their skin, the wrinkles
holding sweet amber smells. We have slept fitfully under the eyes of
slavers, and later watched weary sunsets among the red bricks of cold
cities where the north wind rusts the wood and tears its steel-sharp
claws into the doors. On hungry nights, we lay naked, listening to the
sound of rats and lice scurrying about in the dark.
I have tamed the flames of my body to get food for my man, auctioned its lust to
keep his mask of manhood in place, smiled as I lay with strangers so
that he would never know loneliness. And when he left me, I reshaped
the images of Theallus into new songs. In the hot days of Harlem, I
sang in rat-hole bars. I was Chelsea and Bessie, blues and gospel,
heroin in the blood and coke in the nostrils. I have buried my babies
in swamplands and under cottonwood trees. I have kissed off my men
like forgotten toys and spent my motherhood in kitchens suckling
babies who were not mine.
I brought dark songs to piss-stained hallways, aborted unnamed children in cluttered
alleys, and loved diseased men. I have sweated under the smoothness
of my sister's flesh, driving her into full heat like the demon I am,
tasted the sweet sperm from my brother's penis, and rose from both beds
refreshed and without guilt. I have watched hate dance against black
skin, turning and jumping just so, watched it sleep on the sidewalks
of Frisco and wake to the tune of Jim Crow.
Today I walk into hurried streets where exhaust-fumed faces of so-called world
travelers are as pale as the mountains they have fled. They speak

to me with voices like stone against stone. I answer in words stolen
from the dark underside of the brightly plumed touraco. I have sold my
secrets to survive. I am Diamonane, beloved daughter, bird child
of obsidian and serpent. I am the egg, the sperm.

Bone Flames

In a city full of graffiti
Someone finally has found your heartline.
A spray of red announces: *THE URGE TO BUY*
TERRORIZES YOU and you wonder how long
You've been showing your secret vice.
You remember when sales followed seasons
But now seasons seem created for sales
And you always know when one is in progress.
The city grows urgent with numbers baiting you
For once-a-year clearance, closeouts, or two-
For-one for a limited time only,
Liquidations that will hopefully
Get you a dozen items to stave off mortality.

One line spray-painted on a concrete wall
And you feel mugged by graffiti.
You begin to doubt yourself—
Your body is black putty and can be rolfed
Accordingly with fewer cavities,
So you never pass up any possibilities.
You want double or nothing:
Two sets of lungs for the ones now failing,
A heart to replace what floats inside your chest.
You have been weaned into believing everything
In this city is invention and chance finding,
Yet you know delirium is not just a disease of the night.
Buying is what keeps you from thinking about death
And endless tomorrows you can't buy despite
Annual discounts, trade-ins, bargains and rebates.
Even now as everyone around you slips into poverty,

There are warehouses full of material waiting for delivery:
Someone is sewing on a collar or a zipper,
Polishing the base of a lamp like a favorite
Hunting rifle and as long as there are shops
In Vermont and Tibet, you will want all that you see.
You are bent on becoming the things you own,
Indestructible and recycled on instant replay,
The next chapter in a serialized novel.
You refuse to realize that like all of us
You become what you eat:
Life put together with a little paste,
Smuts, molds, fungus and yeast—
And a body that will never forgive you for this.

Where Apartheid Folds into a Wall of Rooms

Between homeland and Cape Town the only free road is sky.
We bury the house each morning and dig it up every night
But without regard to black or white, the sky blinks open
To the same light. At first wink I have already tied walls
To canvas and wind has swallowed that pocket of warmth I call bed.

We have learned to depend on nothing more than sky—
Before dawn I disassemble these bits of rags and metal
We call home in less time than it takes to bind
A child to my back. At dusk we shake Crossroads' dirt
From roof poles, canvas, corrugated tin—a house resurrected
And under the mantle of night grown to family again.

The children know where everything goes. How to avoid
The policeman's stick. A sling for the twins to sleep like black
Seeds of cassavas. Folding chairs and table next to the stove and ready
For water my sons have primed from the squatters' rusty pipe—
If we're lucky dried meat to help gari and coffee make a meal.

If we're lucky the sky will hide us like black dots in night's
Shadows and we will dream about Bantustan and lost kingdoms.
Last April police cracked our thin dreams like twigs on Nsuze River—
They came on a sliver of the new moon to leave me without house
Or husband. I slept in the ruins for seven months to see him safe.

Without this place he would have to burrow under the dark sky of earth
Owning no more than hunger and blood because he is black,
And I'd live less than a slave waiting six months of days alone
In Ciskei's meager sands. But here we've no more than a miner's poor
Luck and a family's hope. The oldest, at the crèche, washes diapers
For the rich while the youngest hides among dying thornbush shadows.

If the sky is not unkind, on good days we keep time until dark.
My sons walk their father safely to stingy work at the factory
Where he bakes biscuits he will never taste under this sky,
And I brew shanty beer, the yeasty smoke driving my thirst
To tears. My love and I are both tempted to own what we make—

Flat bread or beer, babies or cardboard hut, our lives
Cut by whites into pieces like debris and as easily pulled apart
As what we call family. We are in a cycle of battered nights full
Of violent days that tell us when to breathe. We bury everything
Like loose grain or yams. Roof, bed, cups, peace of mind or starving

Babies all returned to sand and waiting that brings us to broken
Dreams, the road that is the skin of dust we travel without
Papers or answers. We draw sun into night as surely as the storm
Washes what we know toward the sea. But each time we reach the moon
We find they have moved heaven to a farther hill.

It Ain't Blues That Blows an Ill Wind

Valaida Snow: Circa 1930

my wish . . . o to be a dragon
a symbol of the power of heaven
of silkworm size . . .
        —Marianne Moore, "O to be a Dragon"

Your bold voice and the light suspended above a trumpet,
Golden as the world-full season of new-blue jazz
That sported you to Europe's sport of kings and dandies—
You caught the last of that royal light and folks
Who boop-de-dooed as if the endless sky were home,
And you a name like wind, a bird flown out of hand.

Valaida, five-note sheets of sound shaped by your hand.
You a blackbird righteously swinging low on a mean trumpet,
In your voice the loose glue of prewar years and home
Any crazy route from here to China that followed jazz—
Honey, your sweet lips razz-ma-tazzed all kinds of folks,
Brown sugar that made them believe the world was dandy.

Backstage you ached along with all those other dancing dandies
Who needed one more footlight and rooms of noisy hands
To make them forget hard times leeching land and home folks—
Oh chile, the time was ripe for Queen Wilhelmina's trumpet,
Long notes held longer than any man as you jazzed
Up the stage, seven pairs of shoes to carry you home.

Girl, they loved your dance of the seven shoes back home.
Your soft shoe, tap, adagio, high-hat rhythms swell and dandy,
But war owns no stage for the good life and all that jazz—
This time the Man goose-stepped with swastika and iron hand
Booking you in a death camp without Wilhelmina's golden trumpet,
And no one there to say European wars ever took black folks.

Blackbirds 1934 and Chocolate Dandies still remembered by folks,
While the world was intently going to hell in a basket and homes
Burned hotter than any blues you wailed on that golden trumpet—
A war chasing sane men from the crowds of gin-roaring dandies
With leaflets claiming the world as the new Germany in each hand,
15 lashes a day and a mandate ending your beloved age of jazz.

Your scat-beat and spiffy voice almost died when jazz
Was lost in a world turned deaf to Jews, Blacks, and nonwhite folks.
Upside down this life, you nearly forgot the feel of trumpet in hand.
3 years' camp left 74 pounds before the *SS Gripsholm* took you home
But the last thing they take is memory, the silky feel of trumpet—
Girl, you owned the music, the uncommon furs, cars and royal dandies.

Valaida, Queen of the Trumpet, of hot snow, hotcha, and hot jazz—
Little Louis of the dandies, your sassy voice made you one of the folks,
Welcomed home from a sky unmistakably dark, blacker ever than your hands.

Juan de Pareja

The arrogant chin and black
diamond eyes telegraph
a sense of not belonging anywhere,
so I fall in love almost too easily
with this 17th-century slave courtier.
He rules this canvas, the sky behind him
caught at the right moment of no gravity
and beneath his thick crimped hair, a cape
falling reluctantly from his shoulders
in a shade of slate too old to fit
the colors I know.

Even he is unfittingly soft for what life
he might have been allowed.
He knows Diego paints him for the color,
no matter that his Moroccan
skin can hide both sorrow and blush.
This morning's run with the dogs
drew dangerously close to hunting
and though he knows a bed of sweet straw
better than a cobbled court,
he must still do tricks for his meat
and grunt to show his pleasure.

Just within his range of vision, sketchily
a window holds the spires of the Basilica
where Cardinal Velasco has threatened to sell
him at least a dozen times this winter
if the master does not paint royal faces
even more regal than they imagined.
Today is market day and he tries not
to think of being sold again in shackles;
the smell of horses thickens the air
but the light is right so he sits still
for a portrait that will be bought centuries
later at a hundred times more
than the price ever paid for his life.

Juan, they are still selling you for millions
and me for scenery while I stare too long
at this painter's dream of reality and illusion.
With a face like that of some neighborhood boy
I've loved, you seem caught between a delicate
sense of light and color however unreal,
your smile a scab that has healed
for the moment over some wound
still raw underneath or the master's
choice of venison perhaps,
or some error in paint for the royal dwarf,
a pigment for your Lady's veil,
her throat pulsing at the spur
of the moment on yet another canvas

where you will never sign your name.
But now your only concern is that bitter-
sweet pose of playing the African gallant,
and how to keep your face from growing
too handsome in a country
where courtyards stink of dog shit and mold
and most men have faces like algae.
I would wish you out of that Moorish
kingdom turned Spanish, pull you from
your slave-bound history into my own
where you can take your rein and become
my cavalier with your all-knowing eyes
and urban smile, with your cape spilling
in velvet folds, heartsblood red and waiting.

Looking for a Country under Its Original Name

gold will not buy this voyage
and I am but a turning point
a teller of tales who wants all the secrets
but none of the answers
who cries and laughs her way through church
meetings, back rooms, undertaker parlors
behind beauty parlors full of card
players, gin drinkers and good women
who would just as soon cut you another hole
before they'd let you sass grown folks
and now me grown
and waiting to see what furrows
I have turned to line my face
when my children finally remember
to call home

and if you ask yourself why this information
is so freely given
remember it wasn't freely earned
and that this is how I always find
my way home even before I have arrived
and that these words hold more than all
the photographs I can remember
and although you may think I travel
these roads for your pleasure
each one brings me closer to where I am
than all the details in the wide-eyed
picture of my mother at eight
sitting between her younger brother
and now dead sister with her father's
hawk-eyed stare pinning them all

on the horizon of the camera's eye
or how I now must squint into a waxy copy
of a daguerreotype holding a young girl
who is to be my mother's mother
and who dressed for the occasion
holds fast to the tight blackness
of her skin and the tight kinks

of thick hair piled neatly
into a coil that all
but hides the fake landscape
backdropped behind her
flat and void of sunlight
which is strange yet familiar
as if I've been there before and know
just what is around the next corner

and finally the journey is so easy
you need only prime me with a bit of buttered bread
to find my family
I will unearth them for you as quickly as a strip
miner might tear that hill you're looking at now
and like the earth they will turn up raw
wood brown and blackened by lime and salt
from seas that no longer exist
though I have often wished this weren't so automatic
the lava and loam
of my bearings rising so quickly to the surface
the bloodlines veined so neatly to their source
their mysteries so perfect even their undoings
seem as planned as way signs on a map

The Olive Trees of Soller

you must always remember that this is an island
and that these people can only remember
the words for how many and when
that in this quagmire of passageways and cobblestones
horses trot toward towns that no longer exist
except on postcards
and without the tour buses this plaza
would never hold the secrets
of the greengrocer's daughter
and that these roads run from right to left
and upside down into both mountains and ocean
and that this cave once held the charred

remains of three thousand Moors
for whom my black heart still hurts
and that these trees though imported
cannot be included on any declaration
that they spitefully grow away
from earth and rock in brutal
grinding spirals as if they have been pulled
from the nightmares of creatures
drawn by Chaka, Tolkien and Sendak
that during movement or sleep
they resemble bones, blood vessels, organs
twisting mean, niggling and arthritic
tearing their way toward an uncanny blue sky
their expulsion from these gardens
caused by light and heat
by excess, overuse
and the awful knowledge of flesh
and as you pass remember how every point
on the skin is immediately open
to nerve endings
and that we haven't even come to the part
where the car hangs over the cliff

New Poems

Everything Worth Remembering

"Take off your mask
I want to remember your face."
　　　—Richard Hugo, October 1982

What is easiest to trace seems best remembered.
Consider any object: the dime-store toy
You carried on Sundays full of dull memories,
Your first wallet creased to a curve
And empty in your back pocket always.
Friend, with the sweet power to remember,
Look in your trunks of war memories

You put on a brave face, one eyebrow cynically
Raised against the logic of a sterile death.
You taught how to gather feelings through things,
Let us push time back and forth between bed
And chair as if we could replace air gone sour
As an old kitchen sponge with memories
Of how we began, recalling as best we could
Names to trigger geographies of scenes.

Before radio, folks died with memories of families
Still weeping in their heads. It was important
Then to remember any sound that meant life.
Now you fill your head with random sound tracks,
Canned music that sells cars, gum, guns—Muzak
Ballets that refuse to let go of bones and haunt
You with half-remembered lyrics, even when you grow
Heavy as a walrus under the weight of your sorrow.

When pain spilled a second skin across your face,
I remembered the uneven silence of other death
Bed visits and waited behind my surgical mask,
Where death is still just a dream I have,
Where it is easier to forget beginnings
Than to envision how we might end. Ask any mother
Who has misplaced the pain of birthing,
Or doctors who practice no more than sleight

Of hand with life, or ask a poet, who, like you,
Knows what it is to fail at love, and how
Remembering too much of anything is its own
Form of madness. In the recesses of the house
Next door, a sculptor works all night carving
From stone a shape he swears he sees hidden in rock.
The eyes I hide behind gather their own fragments.

Moon, Razor, Eye

the knife that does not draw blood draws heart
through blade instead of blade through heart
this knife is sharper and more polite
it is honed against the broken edge
of soon-only-forever, and the blade
coated with its stickiness of loyalty
and love can be used in public for deeper cuts

the knife that does not draw blood tears love
from its center and draws caricatures
where you drown in your best features
this knife draws ugliness, draws cruelty
and you are the stick figure, full
of the pretty poisons of friends and families
leaving behind trails visible only in the right light
like the silver threads of snails or sea snake tracks
like a thin cloud slicing the moon's single eye

and you wonder how you could have missed it all
how you could have missed a thing that moved so swiftly
inside its own deadly silence while you drank the false warmth
of evenings full of the scent of flowers or the old smells
of schoolbooks, umbrellas, rain slicks moist with what home
was like when life was simple and the only bloodless
scrapes were knees and dreams where you awoke falling
into line behind the leader, the father or mother, the trail
that led nowhere when you were still too young to care

later you learned the names of all the things that hurt
and if the knife shakes you loose of its tip
you will learn to wait for blood only you can see

Where Kitchen Table Clubs Mark the Blues

Winters, I broke windshields to get through the ice, and still
Entertainment was bingo, green stamps, cows with windows from the Ag-College.
Concrete collared the ten-mile stretch of Brush Creek—a sluice—
And the sky above so bad, I believed I could pistol whip the weather.

The state line offered a double city of constant weather and uneven tempers
Resting on the reputations of favorite sons, those bad men
Who made it big by hook or crook, and leaving that outlaw town
With its splendid prairie streets, Brush Creek, Melmac, and summers chock
Full of winged cockroaches that pirouetted mid-air in updraft heat.
Winters, I broke windshields to get through the ice, and still

When Ms. Swift raised her skirts, I scurried past packing house smells
To two kids, two jobs, and what time I had left for night's half life.
Holidays, I waded through dust, or snow capricious as any tornado,
To the fake Spanish Village set by some crazy architect at the edge
Of flat grass where ranch houses whitewashed even the best intentions.
Entertainment was bingo, green stamps, cows with windows from the Ag-College

Carved in their sides by future farmers earning graduate degrees,
Bright boys who'd flood a town just to get a lake that bred typhoons.
In season, flash floods swept easily through the middle of Kansas
City—a path made cleaner by cement lining from the Pendergast political
Pockets—a machine so perfect, it cleaved the town by cash and weather,
Leaving concrete to collar the ten-mile stretch of Brush Creek—a sluice—

A line that marked the show-down for the good folks of that bad town.
That alone was enough to make me believe in weather, and one day,
When humidity beat out temperature, I caught prairie fever and challenged
A twister—me: the black scarecrow at the flatlands entrance to Oz,
Daring winds to do their annual haystack dance across the state line,
And the sky so bad, I believed I could pistol whip the weather.

Birds, Weeping, and Song

our mothers consider
us married though we don't expect
to exchange vows   they ply
us with messages
voices breaking in the wells
of record-a-call sanctums   those modern
day substitutes for front porch stoops
but their cries are still
the same   and we are still
children waiting to be called home
warned that it is getting late
and we must stop the game
we must come back for lessons
on how to behave

our mothers' voices
are recorded at the same pitch
we spin the dial from "answer"
to "message" and mothers are threaded
through our lives with casual
guilt beckoning us toward
consequences   but we are still
by nature truants playing past dusk
squabbling over who is It and who
stole first base or the last kiss
and who is singled out   our mothers'
questions hinge on *single* we expect

and their bags are full of guilt
they are full of the same meanings
those two women   tones learned
in separate neighborhoods where home was
a nest of rooms heavy with unspoken words
our messages are too honest for this:
a simple declaration of separate
names and single place is what we've earned
a quick hello   it's me   good-bye
with fragmented musical accompaniment
like oboes caught in errant bursts of wind
dim signals from passing vessels

a note in a bottle
sent with a patient knowing
there will be no instant reply
the tape is wound and ready
our mothers' sighs hold tension at the end
you say   plug in playback   I say
put on hold all incoming calls:
I hear the wind singing

come away with me   now

Foul Line—1987

Her back in a line straight
As an ironing board
She serves my lunch
And never shows her face
    My companion is right
    For her menu—white and male
    She gives him all her attention
    Reading his every wish
    With careful eyes as she avoids
    My gaze
Nothing personal
But all she sees is color
Black, a shadow, something dark
Near her left hip, the one she rests
Her elbow against when she wrist-
Flicks the plate dead center
On my placemat like a back-
Handed pitcher
    Such a little
    Gesture with all the effort
    Of breeding behind it
    So dainty, the proper flaunt
    Of a Southern girl's hanky
    And all within legal
If not civil limits
    And I wonder vaguely if I might

Have met her in Selma
Or later opposite some other picket
Lines—we're the right age
For such encounters
    And despite laws to the contrary
    Neither of us has ever lost
    Our sense of misplacement
    And can say politely
    We both know how far we've come

What Madness Brought Me Here

Dreaming is my ticket for getting here
An accident of timing, a small gesture,
Like a queenly wave of wrist to wrist to hand to kiss
The love of dreaming into love
Until the heart unlocks and spills upon stark daylight
And the sad-old-young lover whose face no longer matters—
My fifteen-year-old player, my last husband, or grey haired
The same man, no name, just: you
And all of you such a muddle of the same tale,
Last night I fought that bed tooth and nail.

This story wanders from sunset to twilight
Sleep, this part I hate, the dream that tells
Me how I cannot move past your mutter-mutter
Sputter never-meant-to-hurt—
Love you-mumble-darling jazz
And slide into grief easy as a baby's wet thumb.
Soon I awake, the pillow damp with tears and spit,
The bed pulled out and spilled, the night turned by
A wall of shadows trying vainly to be something real.

Comes the part where comfort is only the dream
Of knowing how once again I've been suckered
Into some sad man's story of believing
A line older than dirt. Comes the part where I hope
To bite into a line or two of truth

While the stars above my roof turn to stone,
The streets below to glass, and your body,
With its treacherous valleys, alive in dreams
So real, I buy into them no matter what I feel.

There you are—my high-school gladiator,
My meat-and-potatoes man, my Lochinvar—
Doing me again in a dream-world war
As easily as when you nailed me to this bed.
And I still cannot get it in my head
You are no more real now than you were
When you left your handprint on the door,
Your socks and drawers scattered on the floor.

I know more than one woman has watched
Some fool fold his bread and called it loving,
But I've grown too old for such easy play.
So comes the part where only dreams
Can teach me when to take proper note
Of how to spot the same angle of face and voice—
Some lover who dotes on small things, some
Man who reads the same how-to book of games.

My only complaint is that these dreams come
In retrospect—the sweat of recounting
From beginning to end each departure
When what I need most is reverse action
On a slow-motion loop-track of laughter:
Where I am passenger and conductor, reading
The invisible map of how, where I watch
You leave before I say hello, where sleep
Is a kingdom of ordinary memories
And I know—by heart—the body count of my house
Is insistently: one.

à pied

one shoe on the roadway presents
its own riddle of so much left
unsaid regardless of the condition:
scoured, unpolished and crumpled
like a drunk forever missing the next step
the tongue bent inward like some church
gossip who has said finally too much
and snapped that last accusation in public
the absence of laces or any restraints
and how everyone passing lurches away
from any entanglement

all roads at some time or other
have held a single shoe — the forlorn
reminder of someone careless enough to be trapped
like a teenager in the wash of fast travel
the incongruous one shoe out of step
without foot or wheels or movement
yet so commonplace as to almost
be forgotten by what is missing:
the left leg dangling bare
the child crying to be forgiven or the family
car careening on its mission of terror

one shoe on the road leaves it all
unsaid — the something that lies
without comment or recognition
in the heaviest of traffic or mid-lane
and turned sideways near the center
strip as if waiting for someone
to answer its description
if, as my father would say, the shoe fits
but this thing, so ordinary, cannot be
explained so easily like those strips
of rubber from burst tires

we'd soon as not remember how anyone
like a shoe may be lost in a crowd
or how part of what we know to be our lives

can become a stray digit or decimal point
an unrelated member of a set
yet any child from a divorce can tell
you how it feels to be abandoned midstream
while the family makes a fast break
for the nearest off-ramp—and we've all
heard of the countless armies

scattered like shoes in the traffic of war
along roads where city families once
took their Sunday country outings
but one shoe without ballroom or battleground
can never question the hurry of passing
it bends finally into its own loneliness
and unanswered questions of what might have happened
to its owner or what horror has befallen the other shoe

Never Depend on a Shoo-in Candidate

the prince was a boob who couldn't remember the broad's face
his only clue was a shoe
and then the struggle to remember which foot
and she, taking the advice of her sisters, fell for the trap
as if life were romance of a woman's peculiar parts
some spineless tapping of toes
against a fast-running clock
for which some poor dolt could put the whole kingdom in hock

let's take a hard look at this softhearted myth
here is the prince, standing by the door where his footman
kneels, pillow extended
and those sisters, plotting the ugliness of consequences
while she offers the only ticket that could walk her out of here
a foot too shallow to be the business end of anything
all this needs is a banner reading: What's wrong with this picture?
then someone smart enough to offer the answer

and that's where I come in
not with the chance to try on the boot, no matter how glittery
for this black foot I hold will bear no disguise
even a fairy wand from a lazy godmother could not smooth
a structure so obviously built for Serengeti or Sahara
once in London's airport, I saw my Sudanese kinfolk swathed
in furs: their feet, like mine, flat as boards
but not a prince to greet them as crowds parted before them
the life they preserved was held fast by their own charms
and charwoman or dancer, this is our common share

there is much to be said for a birth without silver
spoon or satin pump
and nothing to be gained by expecting a prince
or the myth of stardust and false words
tossed in the casual magic of a few moments
the whole of this kingdom is a jungle
where mating is mere coincidence of castles built
to crumble around the keeper of the keys
sisters who, too often, are trustworthy only with open envy
trying their damnedest to start another myth
to ferret out the easy life
of golden apples, fine clothes and special books
a uterine world where the prince promises to protect them

For Want of a Male a Shoe Was Lost

in 1944 the fitting room was a fluoroscope where bones
of school-bound children danced inside their caskets
of new shoes like halloween cutouts of skeletons caught

in the silent green frost of x-ray machines—all belly and
mouth ready to suck in feet buttoned-up for the onslaught
of death-dealing playgrounds and arithmetic seating

that brown box was the lasting room where the shape
of shoes was determined by metal forms and how uppers fit
linings and eyelets and groove

always with room to grow—the outsoles like running
boards on a Ford and heels clunky as a horse's hooves
tooled to stand the strain on all parts worn

every fall I walked in someone else's shoes
my discomfort of fit explained by news of a war
or feet that, the shoe merchant said, would last forever

(meaning next winter) with stitches to keep me out
of little slips of tongue—that arch-guard of memory
which, if let loose, readily told the world where I stood

but never with the right fit of merchant's shoe
or style to match my mental picture of elegant slipper
which never matched the fluoroscope's ghostly dancing bones

under that machine even cheap shoes could seem handmade
the man turned the dial until my feet were bleached green
and when mama approved of how they had grown bone dainty

she peeled off dollar bills: one for my father in Normandy
one for an uncle in the Pacific or a cousin's government check
the money folded as tight as those new shoes which dressed

me in eyelets that could not see and tongues tucked
away from naked light while the bony shadows of my black feet
danced all alone—radiating green in the moonlight machine

Confessions of a Woman Who Sucks Baby Toes

my one failing of pen to paper
has always been the foot
with carbon or ink, I try drawing saintly
feet—crowned in corns of sorrow—
veins from toe to heartline a single thrust
or warrior feet—so articulately
samurai, each toe deserves a battle name
and rewards of kingdoms and lovers

my failings are legendary
but Gully, by golly, you had something
there: the truth of the horse's mouth
deserves a wall of feet

I dream desert feet—sand-encrusted
onyx that seem to have been sculpted
from the earth's tears—or the fame
of dancers' feet—arches blistered
like a cocksman's bow and soles
scarred like a gypsy bandit from my love
of flying into sheer leaps of little death
all dancers come to know
at night I count my toes and wonder
how those artichokes of pain
can so blithely bear my past

admittedly they try still to reach
for a fallen pen or napkin
(oh my black beauties, we'll crown you yet)
are these not the feet that longed
to master the alphabet and reached D times
ten, toes curled around pen, before
Mama warned them off with jungle threats
buried there somewhere are baby's feet
like flowers gone bad in bitter soil
the skin smooth and sweet—the tips round
as sugar drops and waiting for a lingering kiss

a child's bare feet still seek my weakness
(yes, I await my grandchildren with bated breath)
babies are best before they discover what's under-
foot and while each lick is still a giggle
and good-bye with no feelings hurt—when pure
pleasure of the foot delights like moist grapes
when the sun makes us all too lazy to speak
and we lie on our backs, honeycombed in sweet
grass that sticks like onion skin and brushes
the base of our naked feet in whispers—
like a sheet caressing the rise of a bare
hip under the musty itch of night—the cup

of body so like the inside curve of a foot
arched, yet hidden—always there
incandescent with desire

The Indian Discoverer on the
Dark Continent of Shoes

if legends appeared every day of the week
we would have no patience with coincidence
but having heard my poems on shoes, you offer
me this tale of finding two in a country where folks
never expect the likes of us to find one line of poetry—
much less two shoes—you rock on your heels and Black
Foot to Sudanese delight in the telling as if this
could make us all believers in possibilities—as if
a poem could lead you to that turn in the woods where shoes,
tossed like breadcrumbs or left by some fleetfooted prince
hurrying to the woodchopper's hut, beckon to the innocent

for, by truth, those of us who are transplanted
should not have stopped for such a transient gift
we know you can't put just any shoe on any foot

yet, you wanderer of lost tribes, offer me, lost
forever from my tribal culture, the gift of recovered thick
soled sneakers, which you say, *lay at cross-purposes*
tongues bedraggled like injured cottonmouths or moccasins
waiting on the road for who knows what spells to be broken
and I watch you wear them like gloves, rocking on your heels
as you tell me how comfortable you feel
inside someone else's mystery, your own history scattered
along more roads than this country's maps will ever offer
I cringe, knowing even in dreams, the shoe is an uncomfortable
thing, for fit or not, each confirms a prison

surely, every shoe carries its mark of past life
and despite their casual discovery, Indian or African
there must have been reasons for two to be lost

listen to the small cries when the outer skin
succumbs to weather—or the right learns
to speak sharply to the left, mimicking
some half-forgotten owner, some other wanderer, who
getting up out of shapes and sorts, said perhaps
run my bath, take those mice from the portico
that pumpkin is an eyesore sitting all bruised
like that in morning-after sunlight

      then rocking back on her heels, she picked up
      the shoes, bright as used keys
      and tossed them through her captor's window

Sweet with Wonder My Feet upon Air

my mother said these feet weren't made for walking
just sedan chairs and palanquins, plenty of sunlight
and pheasant under glass, the feathers still intact
but here I am trapped in a world of shoes, my toes
mutating faster than the timing of any evolutionary clock
Mama said: What did you do before you were born
stand in line twice for long legs then take leftover feet
but I've no real complaint against feet that serve me well
bearing up under the weight of such foolishness as heels
and sandals, sling pumps of single gold threads and husbands
and the feet themselves do not lack their own peculiar charm
albeit flat, they are regular and carry the memory of cadence
dancing, they can pass themselves off as winged
and in bed, they languish and purr like virtual pussy cats
but afoot, they are not

it is difficult to define the actual cause
birth defect: *reluctant feet* does not seem appropriate
for if foot followed function, my family would still be
in the Sudan, rubbing their toes
Hannibal would have set down on that Mediterranean shore
left foot in hand, and let those elephants drown
and Cleopatra, bless her heart, would never have walked
as far as that asp, barge or not

my people have walked miles, shackled one to the other
on feet more horrendous than mine
and my first full-time job of shaving Grandma's corns
surely revealed my genetic origins
since I won't swim and can't fly, I must walk
because as my daddy said: these feet won't fit no limb
and crawling is only for coming into this world

unlike Eliot's Mrs. Porter, my mother would not wash
my feet in soda water whenever the moon
asked me to dance nimble on the sweet air
so I disguise these dainty crocodiles I tread on now
for who better than I to badmouth my feet
while I gather what little cover I can hope for
I don't ask much—the extreme unction
of pure expense and comfort will do as I set
out to collect shoe after shoe in the ultimate search
for my own little handsewn, fur-lined jewel of uncommon
measure, or mirrors to draw your vision to eyes or ears
before I resort to the wonder of Redwing triple A lifts
and limp like a salesman into the sunset with my burden
singing: *Flatfoot floojie with the floy-floy*
my closet behind me lined with boxes of leather and canvas

the three-inch, two-inch torture chambers of blunted
and narrow toes—my personal Borgia inventory
my only hope of growing finally beautiful with shoes

About the Author

Colleen J. McElroy holds a B.S. from Kansas State University (1958) and a Ph.D. from the University of Washington (1973) in cultural linguistics and language arts. She has followed a passion for language through careers as a speech therapist, poet and short story writer, and professor of creative writing, third world and women's literature. "Madness," says McElroy, "is a kind of liquid state that can disappoint, terrify, and delight." *What Madness Brought Me Here* is McElroy's third book with Wesleyan. The first, *Queen of the Ebony Isles* (1984), earned her a Before Columbus Association's American Book Award. For the second, *Bone Flames* (1987), she received the Washington State Governor's Award. She has also received an NEA fellowship and a Fulbright Creative Writing Fellowship which took her to Yugoslavia in 1988. Her other books of poetry are: *Lie and Say You Love Me*, *Winters Without Snow*, and *Music from Home: Selected Poems*. McElroy is the author of two works of fiction, *Jesus and Fat Tuesday* and *Driving Under the Cardboard Pines*. She is a professor of English at the University of Washington and lives in Seattle.

About the Book

This book was composed on the Mergenthaler Linotron 202 in Garamond No. 3. Garamond was introduced in America by ATF in 1919, when their cutting, based on the *caractères de l'Université* of the Imprimerie Nationale, appeared. Many other versions were made by the English and American Linotype and Monotype, by Intertype, Ludlow, and the Stempel Foundry. It has been adapted for phototypesetting, CRT typesetting and laser typesetting.

This book was composed by Marathon Typography Service, Inc., Durham, North Carolina and designed and produced by Kachergis Book Design, Pittsboro, North Carolina.

WESLEYAN POETRY, 1990

LIBRARY OF CONGRESS CATALOGING-IN-PUBLICATION DATA
McElroy, Colleen J.
   What madness brought me here : new and selected poems, 1968–1988 /
Colleen J. McElroy — 1st ed.
      p.   cm. — (Wesleyan poetry)
   ISBN 0-8195-2186-8 — ISBN 0-8195-1188-9 (pbk.)
   I. Title   II. Series.
PS3563.A2925W48   1990
811'.54—dc20   89-37803
                  CIP